Campfire's Burning

A Play

Jean M. Hayward

A SAMUEL FRENCH ACTING EDITION

SAMUEL FRENCH

FOUNDED 1830

SAMUELFRENCH-LONDON.CO.UK
SAMUELFRENCH.COM

Copyright © 1985 by Samuel French Ltd
All Rights Reserved

CAMPFIRE'S BURNING is fully protected under the copyright laws of the British Commonwealth, including Canada, the United States of America, and all other countries of the Copyright Union. All rights, including professional and amateur stage productions, recitation, lecturing, public reading, motion picture, radio broadcasting, television and the rights of translation into foreign languages are strictly reserved.

ISBN 978-0-573-12073-2

www.samuelfrench-london.co.uk

www.samuelfrench.com

FOR AMATEUR PRODUCTION ENQUIRIES

UNITED KINGDOM AND WORLD
EXCLUDING NORTH AMERICA
plays@SamuelFrench-London.co.uk
020 7255 4302/01

Each title is subject to availability from Samuel French,

depending upon country of performance.

CAUTION: Professional and amateur producers are hereby warned that *CAMPFIRE'S BURNING* is subject to a licensing fee. Publication of this play does not imply availability for performance. Both amateurs and professionals considering a production are strongly advised to apply to the appropriate agent before starting rehearsals, advertising, or booking a theatre. A licensing fee must be paid whether the title is presented for charity or gain and whether or not admission is charged.

The professional rights in this play are controlled by Samuel French Ltd, 52 Fitzroy Street, London, W1T 5JR.

No one shall make any changes in this title for the purpose of production. No part of this book may be reproduced, stored in a retrieval system, or transmitted in any form, by any means, now known or yet to be invented, including mechanical, electronic, photocopying, recording, videotaping, or otherwise, without the prior written permission of the publisher. No one shall upload this title, or part of this title, to any social media websites.

The right of Jean M. Hayward to be identified as author of this work has been asserted by her in accordance with Section 77 of the Copyright, Designs and Patents Act 1988

CHARACTERS

Shirleen
Debbie
Monty
Tarquin
Ruth

The action takes place on a campsite in England

Time—the present

CAMPFIRE'S BURNING*

A campsite in England. 7 a.m. in the morning

There are two tents on stage. A large Continental type with an awning is occupied by Monty and Ruth, and their son, Tarquin. A small, two-person tent, inexpertly erected, is occupied by Shirleen and Debbie, two teenaged girls with strong, regional accents. On a small stage the large tent may be suggested by an entrance into the back curtains, with polythene windows added, and the small tent may protrude diagonally into the wings

Monty, a middle-aged, hearty, ex-Public School man, wearing a track-suit, enters from the large tent. He takes deep breathes and does limbering-up exercises, jogging on the spot etc.

A loud shriek is heard from the small tent. Monty reacts but continues to exercise

Shirleen (*in the tent*) Eh! Leave it out! *Do* you mind!
Debbie (*in the tent*) Sorry, I'm trying to get me knickers on.
Shirleen Well, keep your big fat bum on your own side.
Debbie Sorry, there i'nt much room in 'ere.

There are shrieks and giggles and the tent wobbles alarmingly

Shirleen You'll 'ave the bleedin' tent down in a minute! What time is it?
Debbie Dunno.

Pause

Shirleen Bloody 'ell, Debbie, it's only seven!
Debbie Aw, come on Shirl, gerrup now you're awake.
Shirleen Oh sh—shove over then.

The muffled giggles and wobbles continue intermittently. Monty lifts up his tent flap and imitates a bugle blowing Reveille *through his cupped hand*

---

*N.B. Paragraph 3 on page ii of this Acting Edition regarding photocopying and video-recording should be carefully read.

Monty (*through the flap*) Come on, campers, rise and shine! Tarquin! Ruth! Come on, you lazy layabouts!

Tarquin puts a bleary head out of the tent

Tarquin Is it morning?
Monty Sun's up. You're wasting the best bit of the day in there.
Tarquin Yeah.

Tarquin withdraws into the tent

Monty (*through the flap*) Come on, son, get your clothes on. Pull your finger out. Water detail, at the double.

Monty continues to exercise. There is a loud scream from the small tent and a sandal is thrown out of it violently

Debbie crawls out of her tent. She is short, fat and wears glasses and is wearing whatever is the very latest in teenage fashions, which does not suit her

Debbie Whatya doin' Shirl?
Shirleen (*in the tent*) There's somethin' crawlin' in it.
Debbie (*picking up the sandal and shaking it*) Oh yeah, there is.
Shirleen (*in the tent*) What is it?
Debbie An earwig, I reckon.
Shirleen (*in the tent*) Ugh! Stamp on it quick.
Debbie Nah, let it go. They don't 'urt you.

Debbie passes the sandal into the tent. Shirleen, still not visible, takes it and passes out a very small kettle

Shirleen (*in the tent*) Get us some water in that, will you, Deb? Then we can 'ave a drink.
Debbie (*taking the kettle*) Where do I go, then?
Shirleen 'Ow the 'ell do I know?
Debbie (*seeing Monty*) 'Scuse me, mister, is there a tap round 'ere?
Monty Good morning. Yes, it's outside the ablutions block.
Debbie You what?
Monty The washrooms. Near the shop.
Debbie Ta. (*Speaking into the tent*) Eh, Shirl, there's a geezer 'ere says there's a shop. Shall I get some milk and stuff?

Shirleen puts her head out of the tent

Shirleen Yeah, right. Didya bring any cornflakes?
Debbie Yeah, and sugar and Nescaff.

Shirleen Just milk we want then. Got any money?
Debbie Pass me purse out. (*To Monty*) Is this shop open yet, mister?

Shirleen disappears into the tent

Monty Probably not, but if you only need milk I believe they put a crate outside.
Debbie Great. Which way didya say?
Monty Hang on. My son will be out in a minute, I'll get him to show you. First time under canvas, is it?
Debbie You what? Oh yeah, campin'. No, we never done it before.

Tarquin enters from the large tent. He is seventeen and wears well pressed jeans and an expensive sweater. He carries a large water container

Monty Ah, there you are, Tarquin. This young lady is looking for water and milk. Show her where to go, will you? (*He indicates the water can*) Need one of these really, you know. You'll be backwards and forwards all day with that.
Debbie Yeah, you're right.

Shirleen emerges with a purse. She is similarly dressed to Debbie, who has copied her, but Shirleen is slim and very pretty

Shirleen Do get on, Deb, me mouth's like a budgie's cage.
Debbie All right, Shirl, I'm going. This guy's going to show me where it is.
Shirleen Oh. (*She looks at Tarquin*) Tell you what, Debbie, you get that cookin' thing goin', I'll fetch the water meself. (*She takes the kettle and crosses to Tarquin*) Bin 'ere before then, 'ave you?
Tarquin (*pleased, but bashful*) We come every summer actually.
Shirleen Lucky for us we're neighbours then, i'nt it? (*As they exit*) 'Ere, what didya say your name was?

Shirleen and Tarquin exit R

Debbie grins sheepishly at Monty and exits into her tent

Monty (*lifting the flap of his tent*) Ruth! Get a move on, old girl. Need any help in the catering department?

Ruth, Monty's wife, emerges, wearing well-cut trousers and a shirt. She shivers

Ruth Do you want a cooked breakfast?

Monty Rather! Always enjoy the old bacon and eggs in camp, don't we?

Ruth Right, I'll get the food unpacked.

Monty I'll get the table, we can eat out here, don't you think?

Ruth Monty, it's freezing!

Monty Nonsense! Good brisk sea air, give us all an appetite. Going to be some real warmth in that sun, later on.

Ruth Couldn't we stay inside until there is?

Monty First rules of the camp, old girl. Plenty of good fresh air and lots of good plain food. Don't need to tell *you* that, do I?

Monty pats Ruth on the bottom as they both exit to their tent

Debbie emerges from her tent with a camping stove which she tries unsuccessfully to light, as her matches keep blowing out

Monty comes back with a small folding table

Monty erects the table whilst singing snatches of "Oh What A Beautiful Morning". He stops singing on catching sight of Debbie's attempts to light her stove

Too much wind.

Debbie Pardon?

Monty Too breezy there. You need to be on the lee side.

Debbie Yeah? Which one's that then?

Monty There, round the back.

Debbie picks up the stove and goes round the back of the tent

Ruth enters carrying a chair and now wearing a thick sweater. She is just in time to see Debbie leaving

Ruth What on earth was that?

Monty One of our neighbours. Haven't you seen them? Two teenagers came last night just after we did. They must have been on the nine o'clock bus.

Ruth Good heavens!

Monty Now, now, musn't be snobbish, not on a camp site. Two deprived kids from an inner-city area, I should think. Very enterprising of them, do them the world of good.

Ruth I expect you're right, dear.

Ruth exits into the tent

Monty (*following her*) First time campers, of course. Need a bit of help. I don't like the look of those guys in this breeze.

Ruth re-enters with another chair, followed by Monty with a third, which is much too low for the table

Ruth Has Tarquin gone for the water? I could do with a hot cup of tea.
Monty All under control. The other girl went with him. Only had a kettle. Can we spare them a bucket, do you think?
Ruth The other girl? With Tarquin? Does she look like that one? Really Monty, I do think you—
Monty Just showing her the ropes, Ruth. I told you, they need a bit of a helping hand. I don't suppose they'll want to socialise, any more than we do.
Ruth Socialise? I don't know what this site is coming to. We might as well go to Blackpool.
Monty More like Benidorm nowadays, old thing.
Ruth Yes, well, I'm going to start cooking. If Tarquin's not back in five minutes you'd better go and look for him.

Ruth exits to her tent

Tarquin and Shirleen enter R with water and a bottle of milk

Monty (*calling to Ruth*) It's all right, Ruth, he's back.
Shirleen 'Ere, your folks think I've got designs on your body. (*To Monty*) It's all right, I never touched 'im, honest.
Monty (*giving Shirleen an artificial smile*) Come on, old son, your mother's waiting for that.
Shirleen See ya, then, Tarky.
Tarquin Yes—er—see you.

Tarquin and Monty exit into their tent

Shirleen (*crossing L*) Deb, where are you? 'Ere's the kettle.

Debbie comes from behind the tent

Debbie Ta.
Shirleen Whatya doin' round there, then?
Debbie Couldn't get the stove goin', could I? It 'as to be on the lee side.
Shirleen You what?

Debbie takes the kettle and puts it on the stove out of sight

Debbie It's just a fancy way of sayin' out the wind. (*She sits down*) Come on then, Shirl, tell us. What's 'e like?
Shirleen Who, Tarquin? (*She sits down*)
Debbie Eh?
Shirleen That's 'is name, honest.

They both collapse with laughter

Debbie Is it foreign, do you reckon?
Shirleen Nah, it's just what them sort of people call their kids. 'E's only a little boy, really, on 'is 'ols from school with Mummy and Daddy. Bit of a wimp, too.
Debbie Nice lookin' though.
Shirleen I suppose so, in a poncy sort of way.
Debbie 'E looks a bit like that Yank detective on the telly.
Shirleen Which?
Debbie You know, the one where there's all them palm trees.
Shirleen Oh, yeah. Where 'e goes water-ski-ing in them smashin' little tight shorts. 'Is girl-friend's got all that frizzy red 'air.
Debbie Yeah. Looks a bit like 'im, don't 'e?
Shirleen Nah, nothing like. Too skinny, for one thing.
Debbie Bet 'e's got plenty of lolly though, Shirl. Didya see that car? And 'is Mum, last night. She's got ever such nice clothes.
Shirleen (*shrieking with laughter*) 'Er? God, I wouldn't be seen dead in them trousers. Neither would she if she could see round the back.
Debbie Oh yeah, well—she's gettin' on a bit an' that.
Shirleen So's my Mum, but she don't look like that. Takes the same size as me, near enough. I should know, she pinches my clothes on Sat'day nights.
Debbie Well, people like that—they're different, aren't they? Don't suppose 'e'd look at us, anyway.
Shirleen Oh, 'e's bin lookin' at me, all right. But that's all 'e's goin' to do. Not my type. (*She stands*) Come on, let's get this nosh, then.
Debbie (*standing*) I've unpacked the box, Shirl, but we 'aven't got any bowls.
Shirleen Bloody 'ell, are we goin' to eat cornflakes off of tin plates, then?
Debbie Looks like it.

Shirleen and Debbie exit to their tent, giggling

Monty and Tarquin enter and sit at the table, Tarquin on the low chair. Ruth follows, now wearing a coat with the collar turned up and a scarf on her head. She carries a tray and hands out plates of bacon and eggs and cutlery

Monty Ah, just the stuff to give the troops! What do you say, Tarquin?

Tarquin Yes, Dad. Thanks, Mother. (*He picks up his knife and fork then puts them down again*) Would you mind frightfully if I just had toast? I'll get it myself.

Monty Toast? Nonsense, old boy, no energy in that. Besides, your mother's gone to a lot of trouble to cook us a good breakfast. You always enjoy bacon and eggs in camp.

Ruth You do need your protein, darling. (*To Monty*) He's awfully thin, isn't he? I don't think they feed them properly at that school, you know.

Monty Damn well ought to, considering what I'm paying for it.

Ruth Quite.

Monty Plenty of filling grub when I was there. Still give you squashed fly pudding, do they, Tark? And boiled baby on Thursdays?

Ruth No, really, Monty, just look at him. (*She pulls at Tarquin's sweater*) I'm sure this fitted him at Easter, now it's quite loose, just hanging on him.

Monty Now, mother. We don't want too much fuss, do we, old son? The boy's growing upwards, that's all. How tall are we now, Tark?

Tarquin (*miserably embarrassed*) Dunno.

Monty Just like I was at his age, all arms and legs. Going to be a fine, strapping lad in a year or too. Not if you don't get outside that breakfast, though. Eat up, there's a good chap.

Tarquin does so, reluctantly

That's right. Now, what do we all want to do today?

Ruth } (*together*) { Well, I thought I'd—
Tarquin } { Well, Dad, I wondered—

Monty Take it fairly easy, shall we? First day, and all that, don't want to overdo it. How about a stroll along the cliff this morning? Take the glasses and the camera—spot of bird-watching—look at the shipping. Back here for an early lunch, then this afternoon I've mapped out a short walk inland. About four miles for the round trip, that all right with you, Ruth? Not

too far for you? Nip in and get the Ordnance will you, Tarquin?
Show you what I had in mind.
Tarquin (*rising*) Which one, Dad?
Monty The one for this area of course, noodle, the one I brought
with me.

Tarquin goes into the tent

Which one! I don't know about feeding him, I sometimes
wonder if they're teaching him anything. Did you make the tea,
old girl?
Ruth (*rising*) Yes, I'll get it.
Monty No, you sit still, I'll do it. All have to do our bit in camp.
It's your holiday too.

Monty exits to his tent

*Debbie and Shirleen enter from their tent with plates of cornflakes
on to which they pour milk from the bottle. During their conversation they also make coffee from the kettle which is behind the
tent*

Debbie Eh, Shirl, is there a loo round that ablutions place?
Shirleen Yeah, that's what it is. Toilets and wash-basins an' that.
'Aven't you bin yet?
Debbie Nah, didn't fancy them bushes again. Glad we 'aven't got
to do that all the time.
Shirleen Yeah, all them bloody nettles!
Debbie And them mucky cows!

*They both shriek with laughter. Ruth, who is eating her breakfast,
glances across at them*

(*Still laughing but embarrassed*) 'Ere, shurup, Shirl, somebody's
listening.
Shirleen Who? (*She turns to stare at Ruth and does not lower her
voice*) 'Er next door, do you mean? So what? She 'as to go as
well, don't she? 'Ere, Deb, do you think they 'ave a portable
potty in them flash tents? (*In a "posh" accent*) Toilet facilities *en
suite*, folds flat for easy storage.

Debbie and Shirleen continue to eat their cornflakes, giggling quietly

*Tarquin emerges with the map and glances across at them,
wistfully*

Ruth (*in a carrying whisper*) Tarquin, I hope you won't get too friendly with those girls in the next tent. Your father is right, of course, they obviously come from a very poor background. Be pleasant, by all means, but try not to encourage them.

Tarquin I don't think they'll let me.

Ruth What? Yes, well, that's all right then, isn't it?

Monty enters with the tea

Ruth pours out and Monty spreads out the map, the two activities causing some difficulty on the small table

Monty Right. Now, if we follow this brook upstream—you remember this one, Ruth? It gets very pretty further along. Bring your trunks if you like, Tark, we swam there two years back when we had a heatwave, remember? Then we strike out cross country, here, towards this village. What's its name, I can't quite read it?

Ruth (*looking*) Ah yes, there's that rather nice tea-shop, by the bridge.

Monty That's the one. Home-made jam and scones, your favourite, old boy.

Ruth That's right, dear. You ate far too many one year, do you remember?

Tarquin No.

Ruth Oh yes, you do, surely? "More 'cons, Mummy, more 'cons". Your father had to buy an extra plateful because you'd eaten ours as well. Oh, you did enjoy your 'cons! (*Pause*) You were frightfully sick, of course. Do you remember that, Monty? He had some jarmies with Pooh on them. I was washing them out at three in the morning.

Tarquin Ugh! Pooh *and* sick?

Ruth Winnie-the-Pooh, Tarquin. I don't think that's very funny.

Tarquin How old was I?

Ruth About six, I suppose. You were awfully—

Monty Look, can we get on? After that we come back to camp by road. Well, it's just a lane, really, shouldn't be much traffic.

Tarquin More than the odd Austin Seven by now though, Dad.

Ruth You're in a very funny mood, Tarquin. I don't care for it. He's in a very funny mood, Monty.

Monty Bit more respect for your mother then, there's a good chap.

Tarquin Actually, Dad, I was wondering—I thought perhaps I'd have a walk into town some time. You know, on my own—sort of—

Pause. Monty and Ruth sip their tea. Debbie and Shirleen rinse their pots with water from the kettle with much giggling as they spill it on their feet

During the next speeches Debbie and Shirleen both go into the tent with the crockery. Debbie then emerges and exits R with the kettle, towel and sponge-bag

Ruth Have you forgotten to pack something? Do you need to do some shopping?

Tarquin No. I just thought I'd—you know—have a look round. Doesn't have to be today.

Monty Oh, you don't want to do that, old son. We don't go into town unless we have to, do we? Not much there for us. Your mother will tell you the same.

Ruth You wouldn't like it, really, darling. It's all amusement arcades and hamburger stands and far too many people. Of course, it used to be quite pleasant. There were fishermen's cottages down by the quay, years ago. But that was when you were in your push-chair.

Monty That's right. Used to spend a bit of time there when the weather was too bad for buckets and spades. But not since you could walk instead. Oh no, you wouldn't like it at all, old son.

Tarquin Well, I thought I'd have a look. Doesn't have to be today.

Pause

Ruth I daresay we could walk back that way, one afternoon, if he really wants to see it, dear.

Monty Yes, well, we'll see, we'll see.

Tarquin No, that's not what I—

Monty Right, that's settled then. Chores first, then a good blow on the cliffs. Fall in, all hands. We'll wash up, Tarquin, your mother can make the beds.

They begin to clear the table

Ruth If we're not rushing, dear, I think I'll go and have a shower first.

Monty Oh, you don't want to waste the daylight, do you? Have one tonight, I should.

Ruth No, I think I'll go now, dear. The water is more likely to be warm in the mornings. Perhaps the weather will be too, by the time we're ready.

Monty, Tarquin and Ruth exit to their tent. Ruth comes back with a sponge-bag and towel and exits R

After a pause Debbie enters R, *running, carrying her towel and sponge-bag*

Debbie Ay, Shirl, guess what?

Shirleen comes out of the tent

Shirleen What?
Debbie There's a caravan round the other side an' it's full of bikers.
Shirleen Go on, 'ow do you know?
Debbie 'Cause there's all the bikes outside it an' some smashin' guys playin' football in a field.
Shirleen Cor, let's go an' 'ave a look then.
Debbie Do you reckon?
Shirleen Well, it beats sittin' about in a tent, don't it?
Debbie Yeah, you're right. (*She throws her towel and sponge-bag into the tent*)

Debbie and Shirleen exit R, *giggling*

Monty and Tarquin enter from their tent and fold the table. During their conversation they take it and the chairs into the tent

Monty Better get a film in the old camera; the light should be good by the sea.
Tarquin I hope it warms up a bit for poor old Mum.
Monty What? What do you mean by that, Tarquin?
Tarquin Nothing, Dad. Only she's not too keen on cold winds on cliff tops, is she?
Monty Your mother looks forward to this holiday as much as I do. All of us together. Looks forward to it. I hope you're not going to spoil it for her this year, Tarquin.
Tarquin No, Dad, I don't want to do that. It's just—
Monty She misses you, you know, old boy. Likes having you home for the hols.
Tarquin Yes, Dad.
Monty Right. No need to say any more then, Tark?

Tarquin No, Dad.

Monty puts an arm round Tarquin's shoulders to the latter's embarrassment

Monty Women, you know, son, feel these things more than we do. Very easy to hurt their feelings, know what I mean? Have to humour them a bit, now and then.

Tarquin Yes, Dad.

Monty It's going to be a good holiday, then, right? All one happy family, same as usual. So—let's get things ship-shape, then, before she comes back. We'll need more water, old chap, I filled the pan for the dishes.

Tarquin Righto, Dad.

Monty and Tarquin exit to their tent

After a pause Debbie enters R, slowly and very disconsolate

Debbie sits in front of her tent sniffing and twisting her handkerchief

Tarquin enters from his tent with the water can. He sees Debbie and tentatively crosses to her

Tarquin Hello. Are you all right?

Debbie Yeah, I s'pose so. Ta.

Tarquin Where's your friend?

Debbie (*blowing her nose*) She's only gone off with one of them bikers, 'asn't she.

Tarquin Sorry?

Debbie Them bikers. We went to watch 'em playin' football— round there. We 'adn't 'ardly bin there two minutes. This smashin' guy comes over, straight off, and sez, "Right, girl, are you comin'?". An' she gets on the back of 'is bike and they're away. Never even waved, did she, never mind sayin' cheerio.

Tarquin Oh, I say, that's a bit mean. Does she often do things like that?

Debbie (*indignantly*) No, course not. (*Pause*) Well, yes, sometimes.

Tarquin Why on earth do you put up with it? You came on holiday together, after all.

Debbie Well, we're best friends, aren't we? (*Pause*) Besides, some- times she takes me with'er and sometimes 'er friend'll bring a friend, like.

Tarquin Ah yes, I've got a friend at school like that, actually. (*He* *sits beside Debbie*) Not that we meet many girls there, mind you, and if we do, he always gets the pretty one.

Debbie Yeah.

Tarquin Oh, I didn't mean—I mean—looks aren't all that important, are they?

Debbie They are when you 'aven't got any.

Tarquin Mm. Like money, I suppose.

Pause. They both stare in front of them thoughtfully

What do you do, back home?

Debbie Shirl's on the social. I'm doing one of them youth training things.

Tarquin Oh. Well, that's something, isn't it? What do you do?

Debbie Shelf-fillin' at Safeway's.

Tarquin Oh. But what are you training to be?

Debbie A shelf-filler at Safeway's.

Tarquin Oh. Still, you are earning, that's something.

Debbie Yeah. Two quid a week more than Shirl.

Tarquin Oh.

Pause

Debbie What are you goin' to do when you finish school?

Tarquin My parents hope I'll get into University, but I think I'll be lucky if I get into a Poly when I see my A levels.

Debbie Yeah? You'll be lucky anyway, though, won't you?

Tarquin Yes, I suppose so. Some ways. Actually, I've been envious of you, until now.

Debbie Me? You? Garn, you're puttin' me on!

Tarquin No, honestly. You and Shirl seemed to be having such a good time. You know, larking about and not having anybody telling you what to do.

Debbie Oh well, on 'oliday, yeah. You want to 'ear me Dad layin' the law down at home, though.

Tarquin Does he really? But you are away by yourselves, aren't you?

Debbie Glad to get rid of us for a bit, I s'pose. Don't yours let you go anywhere?

Tarquin I don't know really. I'm away at school most of the time. It wouldn't seem fair not to come on holiday with them. One just doesn't ask.

Debbie Well, it's their own look out, in't it? They didn't 'ave to board you out. I mean, it's not like you was in care or gone to Borstal, is it?

Tarquin No, that's true.

Debbie There y'are then. Funny, when you come to think of it. Round our way they moan like 'ell if they get their kids took off 'em. Your lot pay all that money to send theirs away on purpose. 'Ow old were you, when you went?

Tarquin Eight.

Debbie Poor little sod!

Tarquin (*laughing*) That's what I thought, except I didn't know the word until I got there. (*He stands*) Well, I suppose I'd better fetch this water or my Dad'll be laying the law down again. Do you want some? He said something about lending you a bucket.

Debbie Yeah, thanks, might as well come with you.

Tarquin offers Debbie a hand and pulls her to her feet

Tarquin I say Debbie, you're really much nicer than Shirleen, you know.

Debbie Honest? D'ya reckon?

Tarquin Yes, I do reckon. I like talking to you. I was a bit—well—scared, I suppose, of Shirleen.

Debbie Cor! And she said you was a wimp, but you're not neither.

They cross to the large tent

Tarquin Just hang on a minute, I'll get the bucket. (*He hands Debbie the water can*)

Tarquin exits to his tent

Ruth enters R

Ruth is taken aback at seeing Debbie, but graciously polite

Ruth Good morning. Are you enjoying your holiday?

Debbie Yeah, it's all right.

Ruth It's a very pleasant spot, isn't it?

Debbie Yeah, it's all right.

Ruth We come every year, you know. I expect Tarquin told you.

Debbie Yeah, he said.

Ruth It's very quiet, I suppose, for young people, but Tarquin loves it.

Pause. Debbie does not respond

You're new to camping, aren't you?

Debbie Yeah.

Ruth We thought so. (*With a little laugh*) My husband can't wait to get his hands on those guys of yours.

Debbie Oo-er. What guys? D'ya mean them bikers?

Ruth Sorry? Oh no, the guy ropes. On the tent. It is rather saggy-baggy, isn't it?

Debbie Oh yeah. We borrowed it off of Shirl's brother Kev. 'E don't know much about camping either. Used to take it to pop concerts.

Ruth How interesting! And does he not need it this year?

Debbie Nah. 'E's too old. Anyway, 'is girl-friend's in the club.

Tarquin enters with the bucket

Ruth Oh good, you're both going for water, are you? Do ask if you need anything else, won't you?

Debbie Ta.

Ruth That's always been Tarquin's job in camp. He was carrying that old can when he was hardly big enough to lift it, weren't you, dear? "Gungha Din!", his father used to call, and he'd toddle along, so pleased to be useful. Do you remember how proud you were when you first managed to bring it back full to the brim?

Tarquin Not really, Mother, no. Mother, this is Debbie.

Ruth Yes, we've been chatting. Your friend isn't with you, then?

Tarquin She had to go into town, so Debbie's on her own, Mother.

Ruth Oh, what a shame!

Tarquin Actually, I was wondering, Mum, perhaps Debbie could come with us this morning. Would you like to, Deb? We're only going for a walk along the cliff path.

Ruth Oh, really, Tarquin, I don't think Debbie would find that very interesting, do you?

Debbie Yes, I would.

Ruth Oh. Well then, you'd be very welcome to join us, of course.

Tarquin Come on then, Deb. Won't be long. (*He moves towards the exit* R, *then turns*) We might go into town this afternoon, Mum. OK, Debbie? Bet I can beat you at Space Invaders.

Debbie You're on. Great.

Debbie and Tarquin exit R

Ruth But Tarquin, your jam scones ... (*She calls into the tent*)
Monty!

Monty enters from the tent

Monty Hello, old girl. Water hot, was it?
Ruth Monty, Tarquin has asked one of those girls to come with us
this morning.
Monty Has he, by George! The sexy one, or the little fat one?
Ruth Don't be coarse, Monty. The one called Debbie.
Monty Ah, that's the plain one. Shouldn't worry, then, old thing.
Ready for off, are we? I've just got to put a film in the camera.
Ruth Monty, this is serious. He says he's going into town with her
this afternoon, too.
Monty Oh. Sorry about that, m'dear. I thought I'd got through to
him on that one. Bound to come sooner or later, though. Boy's
growing up, needs to strike out on his own a bit.
Ruth Well, yes, if he found a nice friend of his own sort—
Monty Now, now, don't let's over react, Ruth. All we have here is
the old wild oats syndrome. Bit of a holiday flirtation. He'll
forget all about it next week.
Ruth I hope you're right. Imagine introducing that to the Fitz-
jordans! If you don't mind, dear, I think I'll stay here and read
this morning. You can keep an eye on them.
Monty Oh, I say, that's a bit petty, don't you think? Sulking in the
tent, spoiling your own holiday over a little thing like—
Ruth No, I won't be sulking, dear. If you want the truth of the
matter, (*with rising spirit*), I would far rather be reading my
library book than hanging around on a draughty cliff, gazing at
gannets and specks on the horizon that might, or might not be,
f-frigates. And if Tarquin doesn't need my company, I shall
please myself at last.

Ruth makes a sweeping exit into the tent

*Monty stares after her, registering first bewilderment, then hurt
feelings. Finally, his face lights up and he lifts the tent-flap*

Monty Tell you what, old girl, if everybody else is accounted for, I
might get in a round of golf before lunch.

CURTAIN

FURNITURE AND PROPERTY LIST

On stage: One large tent (Continental style)
One small two-person tent

Off stage: IN LARGE TENT
Large water container **(Tarquin)**
Folding table **(Monty)**
Two camping chairs **(Ruth)**
One low chair **(Monty)**
Tray. *On it:* three plates of egg and bacon, cutlery **(Ruth)**
Ordnance map **(Tarquin)**
Tray. *On it:* pot of tea, three mugs, milk, sugar, spoons **(Monty)**
Towel, sponge-bag **(Ruth)**
Bucket **(Tarquin)**

IN SMALL TENT
Sandal **(Shirleen)**
Kettle **(Shirleen)**
Purse **(Shirleen)**
Camping stove **(Debbie)**
Matches **(Debbie)**
Plates of cornflakes **(Debbie and Shirleen)**
Coffee, 2 mugs, spoon **(Debbie and Shirleen)**
Towel, sponge-bag **(Debbie)**

Bottle of milk **(Shirleen)**

Personal: **Debbie:** handkerchief

LIGHTING PLOT

One exterior setting. No practical fittings required

To open: early morning light, increasing in intensity during
      play

No cues

EFFECTS PLOT

No specific cues, but background atmosphere to indicate the countryside/ seaside may be used

MADE AND PRINTED IN GREAT BRITAIN BY
LATIMER TREND & COMPANY LTD, PLYMOUTH
MADE IN ENGLAND

www.ingramcontent.com/pod-product-compliance
Ingram Content Group UK Ltd.
Pitfield, Milton Keynes, MK11 3LW, UK
UKHW021819150726
7214IPUK00017B/199